Gratitude Journal

*With Prompts and Affirmations
for reflection, mindfulness and positivity*

CAMPTYS INSPIRATIONS

Pocket Learner Publishing

Thank you for choosing this coloring journal

If you like this book I'd really appreciate it if you'd leave me a review and have a look at my other books.

Gratitude Journal

With Prompts and Affirmations
for reflection, mindfulness and positivity

© Copyright Camptys Inspirations - All rights reserved.

The content contained in this book may not be reproduced, duplicated or transmitted without direct written permission from the author or publisher.

ISBN:978-1-914997-31-0 (sc)   978-1-914997-32-7 (hc)

Pocket Learner Publishing

A Gift for You

Please join our mailing list to receive periodic updates and materials. You'll also be able to keep abreast of our future publications.

As a thank you please visit the following page or scan the QR code to download a set of original inspirational posters that you can print out, frame and position in your favorite space.

http://eepurl.com/h8SU31

Please leave a review

As an independent publisher with a small marketing budget, reviews are very important to us. If you like this material we'd really appreciate it if you could leave us a review on Amazon.

The wonders of gratitude journaling

Gratitude journaling is the practice of taking time to reflect and document those things for which you are thankful and appreciative. The benefits of gratitude journaling have been well established over the years.

There is, therefore, no surprise that this concept is advocated by mental health professionals everywhere as a means of helping individuals achieve happier, better, more fulfilled lives.

Studies have found that the practice of gratitude journaling positively impacts wellbeing. Documenting gratitude empowers you to feel more positive emotions, which helps to build up mental resilience that enable you to cope with and manage challenging situations. It also improves relationships, develops empathy, and reduces aggression.

Gratitude journaling helps clear your mind, allowing you to sleep better. Improved sleep positively impacts the health of your mind and body, thus enhancing your general wellbeing.

Gratitude improves mindfulness. Taking a moment to celebrate small wins goes a long way in boosting your mental health. People who consciously take note of what's working for them tend to be happier and less depressed or stressed.

Expressing gratitude in writing encourages you to focus on what you have rather than what you think you lack. This mindset shift from focusing on what you don't have, to concentrating on abundance, enables you to be more present and mindful. This attitude leads to improved self-esteem as you are less likely to compare yourself with others. When you write down what's going right in your life, you recognise that it's not all bad. This recognition and acceptance create a sense of calm and stability, despite existing external pressures.

Gratitude journaling helps you renew your mind so that it can be clearer to make better choices. In addition, the habit of daily journaling enables you to be more present and mindful as you begin to focus more clearly on the small wins in your day.

When you begin your day by writing in your gratitude journal, it puts you in a positive frame of mind. The practice also enables you to handle the ups and downs you may encounter during the day. When your plans derail, you can cope better because your mind is clear despite the noise and din of contemporary society.

Not to be ignored are the benefits that gratitude journaling brings to relationships. Rather than argue, you write down your thoughts and focus on yourself. These actions have a calming effect as they help you reflect and become a better person.

We present this gratitude journal with the hope that you find it a worthy companion on your recording journey. Please feel free to give us feedback via your reviews or contact us at info@camptys.com. Please also visit our author page on Amazon (camptys inspirations) to see our range of journals and activity books.

This journal belongs to:

_____

Today's Date: _____

MY THOUGHTS ABOUT TODAY

Consider: People, places, experiences, activities, accomplishments, surprises, coincidences, ideas, lessons, inspirations, aspirations, appreciation, hopes, fears, feelings, failings, concerns, health, meals, enjoyment, eureka moments...

_____
_____
_____
_____
_____
_____
_____
_____
_____

Today's Affirmation

Being true to myself matters

TODAY I AM GRATEFUL FOR

1. _____
2. _____
3. _____

TODAY I FELT

HOW I RATE THE DAY

Why I am grateful:

_____
_____
_____
_____
_____

Tomorrow I look forward to:

Priorities:
- ☐ _____
- ☐ _____
- ☐ _____

What I learned today:

Notes to self

Date: _____

Weather: ☀ ⛅ ☁ ⛈ 🌧

Today's Date: _____

MY THOUGHTS ABOUT TODAY

Consider: People, places, experiences, activities, accomplishments, surprises, coincidences, ideas, lessons, inspirations, aspirations, appreciation, hopes, fears, feelings, failings, concerns, health, meals, enjoyment, eureka moments...

_____
_____
_____
_____
_____
_____
_____
_____
_____

Today's Affirmation
Challenges are opportunities to learn and grow

TODAY I AM GRATEFUL FOR

1. _____
2. _____
3. _____

TODAY I FELT

HOW I RATE THE DAY
☆ ☆ ☆ ☆ ☆

Why I am grateful:

_____
_____
_____
_____
_____
_____

Tomorrow I look forward to:

_____
_____
_____

Priorities:

☐ _____
☐ _____
☐ _____

What I learned today:

_____
_____
_____
_____
_____

Notes to self

Date: ....

Weather: ☀ ⛅ ☁ ⛈ 🌧

Today's Date: _____

MY THOUGHTS ABOUT TODAY

Consider: *People, places, experiences, activities, accomplishments, surprises, coincidences, ideas, lessons, inspirations, aspirations, appreciation, hopes, fears, feelings, failings, concerns, health, meals, enjoyment, eureka moments...*

_____
_____
_____
_____
_____
_____
_____

Today's Affirmation

Doing my best is enough

TODAY I AM GRATEFUL FOR

1. _____
2. _____
3. _____

TODAY I FELT

HOW I RATE THE DAY

Why I am grateful:
_____
_____
_____
_____
_____

Tomorrow I look forward to:

Priorities:
- _____
- _____
- _____

What I learned today:

Notes to self

Date: ....

Weather:

Today's Date: _____

MY THOUGHTS ABOUT TODAY

Consider: People, places, experiences, activities, accomplishments, surprises, coincidences, ideas, lessons, inspirations, aspirations, appreciation, hopes, fears, feelings, failings, concerns, health, meals, enjoyment, eureka moments...

_____
_____
_____
_____
_____
_____
_____
_____
_____

Today's Affirmation

Good things take time and effort

TODAY I AM GRATEFUL FOR

1. _____
2. _____
3. _____

TODAY I FELT

HOW I RATE THE DAY

☆ ☆ ☆ ☆ ☆

Why I am grateful:

_____
_____
_____
_____
_____
_____

Tomorrow I look forward to:

Priorities:

- _____
- _____
- _____

What I learned today:

Notes to self

Date: _____

Weather:

Today's Date: _____

MY THOUGHTS ABOUT TODAY

Consider: *People, places, experiences, activities, accomplishments, surprises, coincidences, ideas, lessons, inspirations, aspirations, appreciation, hopes, fears, feelings, failings, concerns, health, meals, enjoyment, eureka moments...*

_____
_____
_____
_____
_____
_____
_____
_____
_____
_____

Today's Affirmation

I always look for the good in people

TODAY I AM GRATEFUL FOR

1. _____
2. _____
3. _____

TODAY I FELT

HOW I RATE THE DAY

Why I am grateful:
_____
_____
_____
_____
_____
_____

Tomorrow I look forward to:

Priorities:
- ☐ _____
- ☐ _____
- ☐ _____

What I learned today:
_____
_____
_____
_____
_____

Notes to self

Date: _____

Weather: ☀ ⛅ ☁ ⛈ 🌧

Today's Date: _____

MY THOUGHTS ABOUT TODAY

Consider: People, places, experiences, activities, accomplishments, surprises, coincidences, ideas, lessons, inspirations, aspirations, appreciation, hopes, fears, feelings, failings, concerns, health, meals, enjoyment, eureka moments...

_____
_____
_____
_____
_____
_____
_____
_____
_____

Today's Affirmation

I am allowed to say "No" to others

TODAY I AM GRATEFUL FOR

1. _____
2. _____
3. _____

TODAY I FELT

HOW I RATE THE DAY

Why I am grateful:

_____
_____
_____
_____
_____
_____

Tomorrow I look forward to:

Priorities:
- [ ] _____
- [ ] _____
- [ ] _____

What I learned today:

Notes to self

Date: _____

Weather:

Today's Date: _____

MY THOUGHTS ABOUT TODAY

Consider: People, places, experiences, activities, accomplishments, surprises, coincidences, ideas, lessons, inspirations, aspirations, appreciation, hopes, fears, feelings, failings, concerns, health, meals, enjoyment, eureka moments...

_____
_____
_____
_____
_____
_____
_____
_____
_____

Today's Affirmation

I am at peace with myself

TODAY I AM GRATEFUL FOR

1. _____
2. _____
3. _____

TODAY I FELT

HOW I RATE THE DAY

☆ ☆ ☆ ☆ ☆

Why I am grateful:
_____
_____
_____
_____
_____
_____

Tomorrow I look forward to:

Priorities:
- ☐ _____
- ☐ _____
- ☐ _____

What I learned today:
_____
_____
_____
_____

Notes to self

Date: _____

Weather: ☀ ⛅ ☁ ⛈ 🌧

Today's Date: _____

MY THOUGHTS ABOUT TODAY

Consider: People, places, experiences, activities, accomplishments, surprises, coincidences, ideas, lessons, inspirations, aspirations, appreciation, hopes, fears, feelings, failings, concerns, health, meals, enjoyment, eureka moments...

_____
_____
_____
_____
_____
_____
_____
_____
_____
_____

Today's Affirmation

I am a fighter

TODAY I AM GRATEFUL FOR

1. _____
2. _____
3. _____

TODAY I FELT

HOW I RATE THE DAY

Why I am grateful:
_____
_____
_____
_____
_____
_____

Tomorrow I look forward to:
_____
_____
_____

Priorities:
- [ ] _____
- [ ] _____
- [ ] _____

What I learned today:
_____
_____
_____
_____
_____

Notes to self

Date: _____

Weather: ☀ ⛅ ☁ ⛈ 🌧

Today's Date: _____

MY THOUGHTS ABOUT TODAY

Consider: People, places, experiences, activities, accomplishments, surprises, coincidences, ideas, lessons, inspirations, aspirations, appreciation, hopes, fears, feelings, failings, concerns, health, meals, enjoyment, eureka moments...

_____
_____
_____
_____
_____
_____
_____
_____
_____

Today's Affirmation
I am grateful for everything I have

TODAY I AM GRATEFUL FOR

1. _____
2. _____
3. _____

TODAY I FELT

HOW I RATE THE DAY
☆ ☆ ☆ ☆ ☆

Why I am grateful:
_____
_____
_____
_____
_____

Tomorrow I look forward to:

Priorities:
- _____
- _____
- _____

What I learned today:
_____
_____
_____
_____

Notes to self

Date: _____

Weather:

Today's Date: _____

MY THOUGHTS ABOUT TODAY

Consider: People, places, experiences, activities, accomplishments, surprises, coincidences, ideas, lessons, inspirations, aspirations, appreciation, hopes, fears, feelings, failings, concerns, health, meals, enjoyment, eureka moments...

_____
_____
_____
_____
_____
_____
_____
_____
_____

Today's Affirmation

I am in control of my emotions

TODAY I AM GRATEFUL FOR

1. _____
2. _____
3. _____

TODAY I FELT

HOW I RATE THE DAY

☆ ☆ ☆ ☆ ☆

Why I am grateful:
_____
_____
_____
_____
_____

Tomorrow I look forward to:
_____
_____
_____

Priorities:
- ☐ _____
- ☐ _____
- ☐ _____

What I learned today:
_____
_____
_____
_____

Notes to self

Date: ....

Weather: ☀ ⛅ ☁ ⛈ 🌧

Today's Date: _____

MY THOUGHTS ABOUT TODAY

Consider: People, places, experiences, activities, accomplishments, surprises, coincidences, ideas, lessons, inspirations, aspirations, appreciation, hopes, fears, feelings, failings, concerns, health, meals, enjoyment, eureka moments...

_____
_____
_____
_____
_____
_____
_____
_____
_____
_____

Today's Affirmation
I am neither below nor above anyone else

TODAY I AM GRATEFUL FOR

1. _____
2. _____
3. _____

TODAY I FELT

HOW I RATE THE DAY

Why I am grateful:
_____
_____
_____
_____
_____
_____

Tomorrow I look forward to:

Priorities:
- ☐ _____
- ☐ _____
- ☐ _____

What I learned today:

Notes to self

Date: _____

Weather:

Today's Date: _____

MY THOUGHTS ABOUT TODAY

Consider: People, places, experiences, activities, accomplishments, surprises, coincidences, ideas, lessons, inspirations, aspirations, appreciation, hopes, fears, feelings, failings, concerns, health, meals, enjoyment, eureka moments...

TODAY I AM GRATEFUL FOR

Today's Affirmation
I am open and ready to learn

1.
2.
3.

TODAY I FELT

HOW I RATE THE DAY
☆ ☆ ☆ ☆ ☆

Why I am grateful:
_____
_____
_____
_____
_____

Tomorrow I look forward to:
_____
_____
_____

Priorities:
- [ ] _____
- [ ] _____
- [ ] _____

What I learned today:
_____
_____
_____
_____

Notes to self

Date: _____

Weather: ☀ ⛅ ☁ ⛈ 🌧

Today's Date: _____

MY THOUGHTS ABOUT TODAY

Consider: People, places, experiences, activities, accomplishments, surprises, coincidences, ideas, lessons, inspirations, aspirations, appreciation, hopes, fears, feelings, failings, concerns, health, meals, enjoyment, eureka moments...

_____
_____
_____
_____
_____
_____
_____
_____
_____

TODAY I AM GRATEFUL FOR

Today's Affirmation

I am perfect just the way I am

1. _____
2. _____
3. _____

TODAY I FELT

HOW I RATE THE DAY

☆ ☆ ☆ ☆ ☆

Why I am grateful:
_____
_____
_____
_____
_____

Tomorrow I look forward to:

Priorities:
- ☐ _____
- ☐ _____
- ☐ _____

What I learned today:
_____
_____
_____
_____

Notes to self

Date: _____

Weather: ☀ ⛅ ☁ ⛈ 🌧

Today's Date: _____

MY THOUGHTS ABOUT TODAY

Consider: People, places, experiences, activities, accomplishments, surprises, coincidences, ideas, lessons, inspirations, aspirations, appreciation, hopes, fears, feelings, failings, concerns, health, meals, enjoyment, eureka moments...

_____
_____
_____
_____
_____
_____
_____
_____
_____
_____

Today's Affirmation

I am resilient -
I get through
difficulties if I stay
focused

1. _____
2. _____
3. _____

TODAY I FELT

HOW I RATE THE DAY

Why I am grateful:
_____
_____
_____
_____
_____

Tomorrow I look forward to:
_____
_____
_____

Priorities:
☐ _____
☐ _____
☐ _____

What I learned today:
_____
_____
_____
_____

Notes to self

Date: _____

Weather: ☀ ⛅ ☁ ⛈ 🌧

Today's Date: _____

MY THOUGHTS ABOUT TODAY

Consider: People, places, experiences, activities, accomplishments, surprises, coincidences, ideas, lessons, inspirations, aspirations, appreciation, hopes, fears, feelings, failings, concerns, health, meals, enjoyment, eureka moments...

_____
_____
_____
_____
_____
_____
_____
_____
_____

Today's Affirmation

I am unique and I have a unique purpose

TODAY I AM GRATEFUL FOR

1. _____
2. _____
3. _____

TODAY I FELT

HOW I RATE THE DAY

Why I am grateful:
_____
_____
_____
_____
_____

Tomorrow I look forward to:

Priorities:
- ☐ _____
- ☐ _____
- ☐ _____

What I learned today:

Notes to self

Date: _____

Weather: ☀ ⛅ ☁ ⛈ 🌧

Today's Date: _____

MY THOUGHTS ABOUT TODAY

Consider: People, places, experiences, activities, accomplishments, surprises, coincidences, ideas, lessons, inspirations, aspirations, appreciation, hopes, fears, feelings, failings, concerns, health, meals, enjoyment, eureka moments...

_____
_____
_____
_____
_____
_____
_____
_____
_____

Today's Affirmation

I am worthy of a happy life

TODAY I AM GRATEFUL FOR

1. _____
2. _____
3. _____

TODAY I FELT

HOW I RATE THE DAY

☆ ☆ ☆ ☆ ☆

Why I am grateful:

_____
_____
_____
_____
_____

Tomorrow I look forward to:

Priorities:
- _____
- _____
- _____

What I learned today:
_____
_____
_____
_____

Notes to self

Date: _____

Weather: ☀ ⛅ ☁ ⛈ 🌧

Today's Date: _____

MY THOUGHTS ABOUT TODAY

Consider: *People, places, experiences, activities, accomplishments, surprises, coincidences, ideas, lessons, inspirations, aspirations, appreciation, hopes, fears, feelings, failings, concerns, health, meals, enjoyment, eureka moments...*

_____
_____
_____
_____
_____
_____
_____
_____
_____
_____

Today's Affirmation

I attract abundance into my life

TODAY I AM GRATEFUL FOR

1. _____
2. _____
3. _____

TODAY I FELT

HOW I RATE THE DAY

☆ ☆ ☆ ☆ ☆

Why I am grateful:
_____
_____
_____
_____
_____
_____

Tomorrow I look forward to:

Priorities:
- _____
- _____
- _____

What I learned today:

Notes to self

Date: _____

Weather: ☀ ⛅ ☁ ⛈ 🌧

Today's Date: _____

MY THOUGHTS ABOUT TODAY

Consider: People, places, experiences, activities, accomplishments, surprises, coincidences, ideas, lessons, inspirations, aspirations, appreciation, hopes, fears, feelings, failings, concerns, health, meals, enjoyment, eureka moments...

_____
_____
_____
_____
_____
_____
_____
_____

Today's Affirmation

I believe in myself

TODAY I AM GRATEFUL FOR

❶ _____
❷ _____
❸ _____

TODAY I FELT

HOW I RATE THE DAY
☆ ☆ ☆ ☆ ☆

Why I am grateful:
_____
_____
_____
_____
_____
_____

Tomorrow I look forward to:

Priorities:
- [ ] _____
- [ ] _____
- [ ] _____

What I learned today:
_____
_____
_____
_____
_____

Notes to self

Date: ....

Weather: ☀ ⛅ ☁ ⛈ 🌧

Today's Date: _____

MY THOUGHTS ABOUT TODAY

Consider: People, places, experiences, activities, accomplishments, surprises, coincidences, ideas, lessons, inspirations, aspirations, appreciation, hopes, fears, feelings, failings, concerns, health, meals, enjoyment, eureka moments...

_____
_____
_____
_____
_____
_____
_____
_____

Today's Affirmation

I can always find ways to improve

TODAY I AM GRATEFUL FOR

1. _____
2. _____
3. _____

TODAY I FELT

HOW I RATE THE DAY

☆ ☆ ☆ ☆ ☆

Why I am grateful:

_____
_____
_____
_____
_____

Tomorrow I look forward to:

Priorities:
- ☐ _____
- ☐ _____
- ☐ _____

What I learned today:

Notes to self

Date: _____

Weather: ☀ ⛅ ☁ ⛈ 🌧

Today's Date: _____

MY THOUGHTS ABOUT TODAY

Consider: *People, places, experiences, activities, accomplishments, surprises, coincidences, ideas, lessons, inspirations, aspirations, appreciation, hopes, fears, feelings, failings, concerns, health, meals, enjoyment, eureka moments...*

_____
_____
_____
_____
_____
_____
_____
_____
_____
_____

Today's Affirmation
I can do anything I put my mind to

TODAY I AM GRATEFUL FOR

1. _____
2. _____
3. _____

TODAY I FELT

HOW I RATE THE DAY
☆ ☆ ☆ ☆ ☆

Why I am grateful:
_____
_____
_____
_____
_____
_____

Tomorrow I look forward to:
_____
_____
_____

Priorities:
☐ _____
☐ _____
☐ _____

What I learned today:
_____
_____
_____
_____

Notes to self

Date: _____

Weather: ☀ ⛅ ☁ ⛈ 🌧

Today's Date: _____

MY THOUGHTS ABOUT TODAY

Consider: *People, places, experiences, activities, accomplishments, surprises, coincidences, ideas, lessons, inspirations, aspirations, appreciation, hopes, fears, feelings, failings, concerns, health, meals, enjoyment, eureka moments...*

TODAY I AM GRATEFUL FOR

Today's Affirmation
I can get through anything

1. _____
2. _____
3. _____

TODAY I FELT

HOW I RATE THE DAY
☆ ☆ ☆ ☆ ☆

Why I am grateful:

_____
_____
_____
_____
_____
_____

Tomorrow I look forward to:

Priorities:
- [ ] _____
- [ ] _____
- [ ] _____

What I learned today:

Notes to self

Date: _____

Weather: ☀ ⛅ ☁ ⛈ 🌧

Today's Date: _____

MY THOUGHTS ABOUT TODAY

Consider: People, places, experiences, activities, accomplishments, surprises, coincidences, ideas, lessons, inspirations, aspirations, appreciation, hopes, fears, feelings, failings, concerns, health, meals, enjoyment, eureka moments...

_____
_____
_____
_____
_____
_____
_____
_____

Today's Affirmation
I can make a difference

TODAY I AM GRATEFUL FOR
1. _____
2. _____
3. _____

TODAY I FELT

HOW I RATE THE DAY
☆ ☆ ☆ ☆ ☆

Why I am grateful:
_____
_____
_____
_____
_____
_____

Tomorrow I look forward to:

Priorities:
- [ ] _____
- [ ] _____
- [ ] _____

What I learned today:
_____
_____
_____
_____

Notes to self

Date: ....

Weather: ☀ ⛅ ☁ ⛈ 🌧

Today's Date: _____

MY THOUGHTS ABOUT TODAY

Consider: *People, places, experiences, activities, accomplishments, surprises, coincidences, ideas, lessons, inspirations, aspirations, appreciation, hopes, fears, feelings, failings, concerns, health, meals, enjoyment, eureka moments...*

_____
_____
_____
_____
_____
_____
_____
_____
_____
_____

Today's Affirmation

I choose to think positive

TODAY I AM GRATEFUL FOR

1. _____
2. _____
3. _____

TODAY I FELT

HOW I RATE THE DAY

☆ ☆ ☆ ☆ ☆

Why I am grateful:
_____
_____
_____
_____
_____
_____

Tomorrow I look forward to:

Priorities:
- ☐ _____
- ☐ _____
- ☐ _____

What I learned today:
_____
_____
_____
_____

Notes to self

Date: ....

Weather: ☀ ⛅ ☁ ⛈ 🌧

Today's Date: _____

MY THOUGHTS ABOUT TODAY

Consider: People, places, experiences, activities, accomplishments, surprises, coincidences, ideas, lessons, inspirations, aspirations, appreciation, hopes, fears, feelings, failings, concerns, health, meals, enjoyment, eureka moments...

_____
_____
_____
_____
_____
_____
_____

Today's Affirmation

I do not compare myself with others

TODAY I AM GRATEFUL FOR

1. _____
2. _____
3. _____

TODAY I FELT

HOW I RATE THE DAY

☆ ☆ ☆ ☆ ☆

Why I am grateful:
_____
_____
_____
_____
_____
_____

Tomorrow I look forward to:

Priorities:
- ☐ _____
- ☐ _____
- ☐ _____

What I learned today:

Notes to self

Date: _____

Weather: ☀ ⛅ ☁ ⛈ 🌧

Today's Date: _____

MY THOUGHTS ABOUT TODAY

Consider: People, places, experiences, activities, accomplishments, surprises, coincidences, ideas, lessons, inspirations, aspirations, appreciation, hopes, fears, feelings, failings, concerns, health, meals, enjoyment, eureka moments...

_____
_____
_____
_____
_____
_____
_____
_____

Today's Affirmation
I do what's right when no one is looking

TODAY I AM GRATEFUL FOR
1. _____
2. _____
3. _____

TODAY I FELT

HOW I RATE THE DAY
☆ ☆ ☆ ☆ ☆

Why I am grateful:
_____
_____
_____
_____
_____
_____

Tomorrow I look forward to:

Priorities:
☐ _____
☐ _____
☐ _____

What I learned today:

Notes to self

Date: ....

Weather:

Today's Date: _____

MY THOUGHTS ABOUT TODAY

Consider: People, places, experiences, activities, accomplishments, surprises, coincidences, ideas, lessons, inspirations, aspirations, appreciation, hopes, fears, feelings, failings, concerns, health, meals, enjoyment, eureka moments...

_____
_____
_____
_____
_____
_____
_____
_____
_____
_____

Today's Affirmation

I embrace new opportunities

TODAY I AM GRATEFUL FOR

1. _____
2. _____
3. _____

TODAY I FELT

HOW I RATE THE DAY
☆ ☆ ☆ ☆ ☆

Why I am grateful:
_____
_____
_____
_____
_____
_____

Tomorrow I look forward to:
_____
_____
_____

Priorities:
☐ _____
☐ _____
☐ _____

What I learned today:
_____
_____
_____
_____

Notes to self

Date: ....

Weather: ☀ ⛅ ☁ ⛈ 🌧

Today's Date: _____

MY THOUGHTS ABOUT TODAY

Consider: *People, places, experiences, activities, accomplishments, surprises, coincidences, ideas, lessons, inspirations, aspirations, appreciation, hopes, fears, feelings, failings, concerns, health, meals, enjoyment, eureka moments...*

_____
_____
_____
_____
_____
_____
_____
_____

Today's Affirmation

I forgive myself for my mistakes

TODAY I AM GRATEFUL FOR

1. _____
2. _____
3. _____

TODAY I FELT

HOW I RATE THE DAY
☆ ☆ ☆ ☆ ☆

Why I am grateful:

Tomorrow I look forward to:

Priorities:

What I learned today:

Notes to self

Date: ....

Weather:

Today's Date: _____

MY THOUGHTS ABOUT TODAY

Consider: People, places, experiences, activities, accomplishments, surprises, coincidences, ideas, lessons, inspirations, aspirations, appreciation, hopes, fears, feelings, failings, concerns, health, meals, enjoyment, eureka moments...

_____
_____
_____
_____
_____
_____
_____
_____
_____

Today's Affirmation

I forgive everyone who has ever hurt me

TODAY I AM GRATEFUL FOR

1. _____
2. _____
3. _____

TODAY I FELT

HOW I RATE THE DAY

☆ ☆ ☆ ☆ ☆

Why I am grateful:

Tomorrow I look forward to:

Priorities:

What I learned today:

Notes to self

Date:

Weather:

Today's Date: _____

MY THOUGHTS ABOUT TODAY

Consider: People, places, experiences, activities, accomplishments, surprises, coincidences, ideas, lessons, inspirations, aspirations, appreciation, hopes, fears, feelings, failings, concerns, health, meals, enjoyment, eureka moments...

Today's Affirmation

I get better every single day

TODAY I AM GRATEFUL FOR

1.
2.
3.

TODAY I FELT

HOW I RATE THE DAY

Why I am grateful:

_____
_____
_____
_____
_____
_____

Tomorrow I look forward to:

_____
_____
_____

Priorities:

☐ _____
☐ _____
☐ _____

What I learned today:

_____
_____
_____
_____
_____

Notes to self

Date: ....

Weather: ☀ ⛅ ☁ ⛈ 🌧

Today's Date: _____

MY THOUGHTS ABOUT TODAY

Consider: People, places, experiences, activities, accomplishments, surprises, coincidences, ideas, lessons, inspirations, aspirations, appreciation, hopes, fears, feelings, failings, concerns, health, meals, enjoyment, eureka moments...

_____
_____
_____
_____
_____
_____
_____
_____

Today's Affirmation

I go after my dreams

TODAY I AM GRATEFUL FOR

1. _____
2. _____
3. _____

TODAY I FELT

HOW I RATE THE DAY

☆ ☆ ☆ ☆

Why I am grateful:

Tomorrow I look forward to:

Priorities:

What I learned today:

Notes to self

Date:

Weather:

Today's Date: _____

MY THOUGHTS ABOUT TODAY

Consider: *People, places, experiences, activities, accomplishments, surprises, coincidences, ideas, lessons, inspirations, aspirations, appreciation, hopes, fears, feelings, failings, concerns, health, meals, enjoyment, eureka moments...*

Today's Affirmation

I have people who love me

TODAY I AM GRATEFUL FOR

1. _____
2. _____
3. _____

TODAY I FELT

HOW I RATE THE DAY

☆ ☆ ☆ ☆ ☆

Why I am grateful:

_____
_____
_____
_____
_____
_____

Tomorrow I look forward to:

_____
_____
_____

Priorities:
- [ ] _____
- [ ] _____
- [ ] _____

What I learned today:
_____
_____
_____
_____

Notes to self

Date: _____   Weather: ☀ ⛅ ☁ ⛈ 🌧

Today's Date: _____

MY THOUGHTS ABOUT TODAY

Consider: *People, places, experiences, activities, accomplishments, surprises, coincidences, ideas, lessons, inspirations, aspirations, appreciation, hopes, fears, feelings, failings, concerns, health, meals, enjoyment, eureka moments...*

_____
_____
_____
_____
_____
_____
_____
_____

Today's Affirmation

I have the power to change my every moment

TODAY I AM GRATEFUL FOR

1. _____
2. _____
3. _____

TODAY I FELT

HOW I RATE THE DAY

Why I am grateful:
_____
_____
_____
_____
_____
_____

Tomorrow I look forward to:
_____
_____
_____

Priorities:
☐ _____
☐ _____
☐ _____

What I learned today:
_____
_____
_____
_____
_____

Notes to self

Date: _____

Weather: ☀ ⛅ ☁ ⛈ 🌧

Today's Date: _____

MY THOUGHTS ABOUT TODAY

Consider: *People, places, experiences, activities, accomplishments, surprises, coincidences, ideas, lessons, inspirations, aspirations, appreciation, hopes, fears, feelings, failings, concerns, health, meals, enjoyment, eureka moments...*

_____
_____
_____
_____
_____
_____
_____
_____
_____

Today's Affirmation

I have unlimited potential

TODAY I AM GRATEFUL FOR

1. _____
2. _____
3. _____

TODAY I FELT

HOW I RATE THE DAY

☆ ☆ ☆ ☆ ☆

Why I am grateful:
_____
_____
_____
_____
_____

Tomorrow I look forward to:

Priorities:
- _____
- _____
- _____

What I learned today:
_____
_____
_____
_____

Notes to self

Date: _____   Weather:

Today's Date: _____

MY THOUGHTS ABOUT TODAY

Consider: *People, places, experiences, activities, accomplishments, surprises, coincidences, ideas, lessons, inspirations, aspirations, appreciation, hopes, fears, feelings, failings, concerns, health, meals, enjoyment, eureka moments...*

_____
_____
_____
_____
_____
_____
_____

Today's Affirmation

I identify ways to contribute and impact.

TODAY I AM GRATEFUL FOR

1. _____
2. _____
3. _____

TODAY I FELT

HOW I RATE THE DAY
☆ ☆ ☆ ☆ ☆

Why I am grateful:

_____
_____
_____
_____
_____

Tomorrow I look forward to:

Priorities:
- ☐ _____
- ☐ _____
- ☐ _____

What I learned today:

Notes to self

Date: _____

Weather:

Today's Date: _____

MY THOUGHTS ABOUT TODAY

Consider: *People, places, experiences, activities, accomplishments, surprises, coincidences, ideas, lessons, inspirations, aspirations, appreciation, hopes, fears, feelings, failings, concerns, health, meals, enjoyment, eureka moments...*

_____
_____
_____
_____
_____
_____
_____
_____
_____
_____

Today's Affirmation

I improve with practice

TODAY I AM GRATEFUL FOR

1. _____
2. _____
3. _____

TODAY I FELT

HOW I RATE THE DAY

☆ ☆ ☆ ☆

Why I am grateful:
_____
_____
_____
_____
_____
_____

Tomorrow I look forward to:
_____
_____
_____

Priorities:
☐ _____
☐ _____
☐ _____

What I learned today:
_____
_____
_____
_____

Notes to self

Date: ....

Weather: ☀ ⛅ ☁ ⛈ 🌧

Today's Date: _____

MY THOUGHTS ABOUT TODAY

Consider: *People, places, experiences, activities, accomplishments, surprises, coincidences, ideas, lessons, inspirations, aspirations, appreciation, hopes, fears, feelings, failings, concerns, health, meals, enjoyment, eureka moments...*

_____
_____
_____
_____
_____
_____
_____
_____
_____

Today's Affirmation

I learn from my mistakes

TODAY I AM GRATEFUL FOR

1. _____
2. _____
3. _____

TODAY I FELT

HOW I RATE THE DAY

☆ ☆ ☆ ☆ ☆

Why I am grateful:

___

Tomorrow I look forward to:

Priorities:
- ☐ _____
- ☐ _____
- ☐ _____

What I learned today:

Notes to self

Date: _____

Weather: ☀ ⛅ ☁ ⛈ 🌧

Today's Date: _____

MY THOUGHTS ABOUT TODAY

Consider: *People, places, experiences, activities, accomplishments, surprises, coincidences, ideas, lessons, inspirations, aspirations, appreciation, hopes, fears, feelings, failings, concerns, health, meals, enjoyment, eureka moments...*

_____
_____
_____
_____
_____
_____
_____
_____

Today's Affirmation

I let go of the past and focus on the present

TODAY I AM GRATEFUL FOR

1. _____
2. _____
3. _____

TODAY I FELT

HOW I RATE THE DAY

Why I am grateful:

_____
_____
_____
_____
_____

Tomorrow I look forward to:

Priorities:
- _____
- _____
- _____

What I learned today:

Notes to self

Date: _____

Weather:

Today's Date: _____

MY THOUGHTS ABOUT TODAY

Consider: *People, places, experiences, activities, accomplishments, surprises, coincidences, ideas, lessons, inspirations, aspirations, appreciation, hopes, fears, feelings, failings, concerns, health, meals, enjoyment, eureka moments...*

_____
_____
_____
_____
_____
_____
_____
_____
_____

Today's Affirmation
I let go of what I cannot control

TODAY I AM GRATEFUL FOR

1. _____
2. _____
3. _____

TODAY I FELT

HOW I RATE THE DAY

Why I am grateful:
_____
_____
_____
_____
_____
_____

Tomorrow I look forward to:
_____
_____
_____

Priorities:
☐ _____
☐ _____
☐ _____

What I learned today:
_____
_____
_____
_____

Notes to self

Date: _____

Weather:

Today's Date: _____

MY THOUGHTS ABOUT TODAY

Consider: People, places, experiences, activities, accomplishments, surprises, coincidences, ideas, lessons, inspirations, aspirations, appreciation, hopes, fears, feelings, failings, concerns, health, meals, enjoyment, eureka moments...

_____
_____
_____
_____
_____
_____
_____
_____
_____

Today's Affirmation

I let no one disturb my peace

TODAY I AM GRATEFUL FOR

1. _____
2. _____
3. _____

TODAY I FELT

HOW I RATE THE DAY

☆ ☆ ☆ ☆ ☆

Why I am grateful:
_____
_____
_____
_____
_____
_____

Tomorrow I look forward to:

Priorities:
- ☐ _____
- ☐ _____
- ☐ _____

What I learned today:

Notes to self

Date: _____   Weather: ☀ ⛅ ☁ ⛈ 🌧

Today's Date: _____

MY THOUGHTS ABOUT TODAY

Consider: People, places, experiences, activities, accomplishments, surprises, coincidences, ideas, lessons, inspirations, aspirations, appreciation, hopes, fears, feelings, failings, concerns, health, meals, enjoyment, eureka moments...

Today's Affirmation

I love and accept myself

TODAY I AM GRATEFUL FOR

1.
2.
3.

TODAY I FELT

HOW I RATE THE DAY

☆ ☆ ☆ ☆ ☆

Why I am grateful:
_____
_____
_____
_____
_____

Tomorrow I look forward to:
_____
_____
_____

Priorities:
- [ ] _____
- [ ] _____
- [ ] _____

What I learned today:
_____
_____
_____
_____

Notes to self

Date: ....

Weather:

Today's Date: _____

MY THOUGHTS ABOUT TODAY

Consider: *People, places, experiences, activities, accomplishments, surprises, coincidences, ideas, lessons, inspirations, aspirations, appreciation, hopes, fears, feelings, failings, concerns, health, meals, enjoyment, eureka moments...*

_____
_____
_____
_____
_____
_____
_____
_____
_____

Today's Affirmation

I maintain an attitude of gratitude at all times

TODAY I AM GRATEFUL FOR

1. _____
2. _____
3. _____

TODAY I FELT

HOW I RATE THE DAY

Why I am grateful:
_____
_____
_____
_____
_____

Tomorrow I look forward to:

Priorities:
- _____
- _____
- _____

What I learned today:
_____
_____
_____
_____

Notes to self

Date: _____

Weather:

Today's Date: _____

MY THOUGHTS ABOUT TODAY

Consider: *People, places, experiences, activities, accomplishments, surprises, coincidences, ideas, lessons, inspirations, aspirations, appreciation, hopes, fears, feelings, failings, concerns, health, meals, enjoyment, eureka moments...*

_____
_____
_____
_____
_____
_____
_____

Today's Affirmation

I'm free to create the life I desire

TODAY I AM GRATEFUL FOR

1. _____
2. _____
3. _____

TODAY I FELT

HOW I RATE THE DAY

☆ ☆ ☆ ☆ ☆

Why I am grateful:
_____
_____
_____
_____
_____
_____

Tomorrow I look forward to:

Priorities:
☐ _____
☐ _____
☐ _____

What I learned today:
_____
_____
_____
_____

Notes to self

Date: _____

Weather: ☀ ⛅ ☁ ⛈ 🌧

Today's Date: _____

MY THOUGHTS ABOUT TODAY

Consider: *People, places, experiences, activities, accomplishments, surprises, coincidences, ideas, lessons, inspirations, aspirations, appreciation, hopes, fears, feelings, failings, concerns, health, meals, enjoyment, eureka moments...*

_____
_____
_____
_____
_____
_____
_____
_____
_____
_____

Today's Affirmation

I release doubts and fears

TODAY I AM GRATEFUL FOR

1. _____
2. _____
3. _____

TODAY I FELT

HOW I RATE THE DAY

☆ ☆ ☆ ☆ ☆

Why I am grateful:

_____
_____
_____
_____
_____
_____

Tomorrow I look forward to:

Priorities:
- _____
- _____
- _____

What I learned today:

_____
_____
_____
_____

Notes to self

Date: _____

Weather:

Today's Date: _____

MY THOUGHTS ABOUT TODAY

Consider: *People, places, experiences, activities, accomplishments, surprises, coincidences, ideas, lessons, inspirations, aspirations, appreciation, hopes, fears, feelings, failings, concerns, health, meals, enjoyment, eureka moments...*

_____
_____
_____
_____
_____
_____
_____
_____
_____

Today's Affirmation

I rise above negativity

TODAY I AM GRATEFUL FOR

1. _____
2. _____
3. _____

TODAY I FELT

HOW I RATE THE DAY

☆ ☆ ☆ ☆ ☆

Why I am grateful:
_____
_____
_____
_____
_____

Tomorrow I look forward to:
_____
_____
_____

Priorities:
- [ ] _____
- [ ] _____
- [ ] _____

What I learned today:
_____
_____
_____
_____
_____

Notes to self

Date: _____

Weather: ☀ ⛅ ☁ ⛈ 🌧

Today's Date: _____

MY THOUGHTS ABOUT TODAY

Consider: *People, places, experiences, activities, accomplishments, surprises, coincidences, ideas, lessons, inspirations, aspirations, appreciation, hopes, fears, feelings, failings, concerns, health, meals, enjoyment, eureka moments...*

_____
_____
_____
_____
_____
_____
_____

Today's Affirmation

I stand up for what I believe in

TODAY I AM GRATEFUL FOR

1. _____
2. _____
3. _____

TODAY I FELT

HOW I RATE THE DAY

☆ ☆ ☆ ☆ ☆

Why I am grateful:
_____
_____
_____
_____
_____
_____

Tomorrow I look forward to:

Priorities:
☐ _____
☐ _____
☐ _____

What I learned today:

Notes to self

Date: _____

Weather:

Today's Date: _____

MY THOUGHTS ABOUT TODAY

Consider: People, places, experiences, activities, accomplishments, surprises, coincidences, ideas, lessons, inspirations, aspirations, appreciation, hopes, fears, feelings, failings, concerns, health, meals, enjoyment, eureka moments...

_____
_____
_____
_____
_____
_____
_____
_____
_____

Today's Affirmation

I strive for progress, not perfection

TODAY I AM GRATEFUL FOR

1. _____
2. _____
3. _____

TODAY I FELT

HOW I RATE THE DAY

☆ ☆ ☆ ☆ ☆

Why I am grateful:
_____
_____
_____
_____
_____
_____

Tomorrow I look forward to:

Priorities:
- ☐ _____
- ☐ _____
- ☐ _____

What I learned today:
_____
_____
_____
_____
_____

Notes to self

Date: _____

Weather:

Today's Date: _____

MY THOUGHTS ABOUT TODAY

Consider: *People, places, experiences, activities, accomplishments, surprises, coincidences, ideas, lessons, inspirations, aspirations, appreciation, hopes, fears, feelings, failings, concerns, health, meals, enjoyment, eureka moments...*

_____
_____
_____
_____
_____
_____
_____
_____
_____
_____
_____

Today's Affirmation

I take time out to focus on my mental, physical and spiritual health

TODAY I AM GRATEFUL FOR

1. _____
2. _____
3. _____

TODAY I FELT

HOW I RATE THE DAY

☆ ☆ ☆ ☆ ☆

Why I am grateful:
_____
_____
_____
_____
_____
_____

Tomorrow I look forward to:
_____
_____
_____

Priorities:
☐ _____
☐ _____
☐ _____

What I learned today:
_____
_____
_____
_____
_____

Notes to self

Date: _____   Weather: ☀ ⛅ ☁ ⛈ 🌧

Today's Date: _____

MY THOUGHTS ABOUT TODAY

Consider: People, places, experiences, activities, accomplishments, surprises, coincidences, ideas, lessons, inspirations, aspirations, appreciation, hopes, fears, feelings, failings, concerns, health, meals, enjoyment, eureka moments...

_____
_____
_____
_____
_____
_____
_____
_____

Today's Affirmation
I talk about my feelings when I need to

TODAY I AM GRATEFUL FOR
1. _____
2. _____
3. _____

TODAY I FELT

HOW I RATE THE DAY
☆ ☆ ☆ ☆ ☆

Why I am grateful:
_____
_____
_____
_____
_____
_____

Tomorrow I look forward to:

Priorities:
- ☐ _____
- ☐ _____
- ☐ _____

What I learned today:
_____
_____
_____
_____

Notes to self

Date: _____   Weather: ☀ ⛅ ☁ ⛈ 🌧

Today's Date: _____

MY THOUGHTS ABOUT TODAY

Consider: People, places, experiences, activities, accomplishments, surprises, coincidences, ideas, lessons, inspirations, aspirations, appreciation, hopes, fears, feelings, failings, concerns, health, meals, enjoyment, eureka moments...

_____
_____
_____
_____
_____
_____
_____
_____
_____

Today's Affirmation

I treat others how I want to be treated

TODAY I AM GRATEFUL FOR

1. _____
2. _____
3. _____

TODAY I FELT

HOW I RATE THE DAY

☆ ☆ ☆ ☆ ☆

Why I am grateful:

_____
_____
_____
_____
_____
_____

Tomorrow I look forward to:

Priorities:

☐ _____
☐ _____
☐ _____

What I learned today:

_____
_____
_____
_____

Notes to self

Date: _____

Weather:

Today's Date: _____

MY THOUGHTS ABOUT TODAY

Consider: *People, places, experiences, activities, accomplishments, surprises, coincidences, ideas, lessons, inspirations, aspirations, appreciation, hopes, fears, feelings, failings, concerns, health, meals, enjoyment, eureka moments...*

_____
_____
_____
_____
_____
_____
_____
_____
_____

Today's Affirmation
I do my best

TODAY I AM GRATEFUL FOR

1. _____
2. _____
3. _____

TODAY I FELT

HOW I RATE THE DAY

Why I am grateful:
_____
_____
_____
_____
_____
_____

Tomorrow I look forward to:

Priorities:
- _____
- _____
- _____

What I learned today:
_____
_____
_____
_____
_____

Notes to self

Date: _____

Weather:

Today's Date: _____

MY THOUGHTS ABOUT TODAY

Consider: *People, places, experiences, activities, accomplishments, surprises, coincidences, ideas, lessons, inspirations, aspirations, appreciation, hopes, fears, feelings, failings, concerns, health, meals, enjoyment, eureka moments...*

Today's Affirmation

If I fall I get back up

TODAY I AM GRATEFUL FOR

1. _____
2. _____
3. _____

TODAY I FELT

HOW I RATE THE DAY
☆ ☆ ☆ ☆ ☆

Why I am grateful:
_____
_____
_____
_____
_____

Tomorrow I look forward to:

Priorities:
☐ _____
☐ _____
☐ _____

What I learned today:
_____
_____
_____
_____

Notes to self

Date: ....

Weather: ☀ ⛅ ☁ ⛈ 🌧

Today's Date: _____

MY THOUGHTS ABOUT TODAY

Consider: *People, places, experiences, activities, accomplishments, surprises, coincidences, ideas, lessons, inspirations, aspirations, appreciation, hopes, fears, feelings, failings, concerns, health, meals, enjoyment, eureka moments...*

_____
_____
_____
_____
_____
_____
_____
_____
_____
_____

Today's Affirmation

It's great to be me

TODAY I AM GRATEFUL FOR

1. _____
2. _____
3. _____

TODAY I FELT

HOW I RATE THE DAY

☆ ☆ ☆ ☆ ☆

Why I am grateful:
_____
_____
_____
_____
_____
_____

Tomorrow I look forward to:

Priorities:
- ☐ _____
- ☐ _____
- ☐ _____

What I learned today:
_____
_____
_____
_____

Notes to self

Date: _____

Weather:

Today's Date: _____

MY THOUGHTS ABOUT TODAY

Consider: *People, places, experiences, activities, accomplishments, surprises, coincidences, ideas, lessons, inspirations, aspirations, appreciation, hopes, fears, feelings, failings, concerns, health, meals, enjoyment, eureka moments...*

_____
_____
_____
_____
_____
_____
_____
_____
_____
_____

Today's Affirmation

It's okay to ask for help

TODAY I AM GRATEFUL FOR

1. _____
2. _____
3. _____

TODAY I FELT

HOW I RATE THE DAY

Why I am grateful:

_____
_____
_____
_____
_____
_____

Tomorrow I look forward to:

_____
_____
_____

Priorities:

☐ _____
☐ _____
☐ _____

What I learned today:

_____
_____
_____
_____
_____

Notes to self

Date: ....

Weather: ☀ ⛅ ☁ ⛈ 🌧

Today's Date: _____

MY THOUGHTS ABOUT TODAY

Consider: *People, places, experiences, activities, accomplishments, surprises, coincidences, ideas, lessons, inspirations, aspirations, appreciation, hopes, fears, feelings, failings, concerns, health, meals, enjoyment, eureka moments...*

_____
_____
_____
_____
_____
_____
_____
_____
_____

Today's Affirmation

It's okay to be different because in reality I am

TODAY I AM GRATEFUL FOR

1. _____
2. _____
3. _____

TODAY I FELT

HOW I RATE THE DAY
☆ ☆ ☆ ☆ ☆

Why I am grateful:

_____
_____
_____
_____
_____
_____

Tomorrow I look forward to:

Priorities:

- [ ] _____
- [ ] _____
- [ ] _____

What I learned today:

Notes to self

Date: _____

Weather:

Today's Date: _____

MY THOUGHTS ABOUT TODAY

Consider: *People, places, experiences, activities, accomplishments, surprises, coincidences, ideas, lessons, inspirations, aspirations, appreciation, hopes, fears, feelings, failings, concerns, health, meals, enjoyment, eureka moments...*

_____
_____
_____
_____
_____
_____
_____
_____

Today's Affirmation

It's okay to make mistakes

TODAY I AM GRATEFUL FOR

1. _____
2. _____
3. _____

TODAY I FELT

HOW I RATE THE DAY

☆ ☆ ☆ ☆ ☆

Why I am grateful:
_____
_____
_____
_____
_____
_____

Tomorrow I look forward to:

Priorities:
- ☐ _____
- ☐ _____
- ☐ _____

What I learned today:
_____
_____
_____
_____

Notes to self

Date: _____

Weather: ☀ ⛅ ☁ ⛈ 🌧

Today's Date: _____

MY THOUGHTS ABOUT TODAY

Consider: *People, places, experiences, activities, accomplishments, surprises, coincidences, ideas, lessons, inspirations, aspirations, appreciation, hopes, fears, feelings, failings, concerns, health, meals, enjoyment, eureka moments...*

_____
_____
_____
_____
_____
_____
_____
_____
_____
_____

Today's Affirmation
My future is inundated with possibilities

TODAY I AM GRATEFUL FOR

1. _____
2. _____
3. _____

TODAY I FELT

HOW I RATE THE DAY

Why I am grateful:
_____
_____
_____
_____
_____
_____

Tomorrow I look forward to:

Priorities:
- _____
- _____
- _____

What I learned today:

Notes to self

Date: ....

Weather:

Today's Date: _____

MY THOUGHTS ABOUT TODAY

Consider: *People, places, experiences, activities, accomplishments, surprises, coincidences, ideas, lessons, inspirations, aspirations, appreciation, hopes, fears, feelings, failings, concerns, health, meals, enjoyment, eureka moments...*

_____
_____
_____
_____
_____
_____
_____
_____
_____
_____

Today's Affirmation

My past is not a reflection of my future

TODAY I AM GRATEFUL FOR

1. _____
2. _____
3. _____

TODAY I FELT

HOW I RATE THE DAY

☆ ☆ ☆ ☆ ☆

Why I am grateful:

_____
_____
_____
_____
_____
_____

Tomorrow I look forward to:

Priorities:
- [ ] _____
- [ ] _____
- [ ] _____

What I learned today:

Notes to self

Date: _____

Weather:

Today's Date: _____

MY THOUGHTS ABOUT TODAY

Consider: *People, places, experiences, activities, accomplishments, surprises, coincidences, ideas, lessons, inspirations, aspirations, appreciation, hopes, fears, feelings, failings, concerns, health, meals, enjoyment, eureka moments...*

_____
_____
_____
_____
_____
_____
_____
_____
_____

Today's Affirmation

The greatest gift I can give myself is unconditional love

TODAY I AM GRATEFUL FOR

1. _____
2. _____
3. _____

TODAY I FELT

HOW I RATE THE DAY

☆ ☆ ☆ ☆ ☆

Why I am grateful:

_____
_____
_____
_____
_____
_____

Tomorrow I look forward to:

Priorities:
- _____
- _____
- _____

What I learned today:

Notes to self

Date: _____

Weather:

Today's Date: _____

MY THOUGHTS ABOUT TODAY

Consider: *People, places, experiences, activities, accomplishments, surprises, coincidences, ideas, lessons, inspirations, aspirations, appreciation, hopes, fears, feelings, failings, concerns, health, meals, enjoyment, eureka moments...*

Today's Affirmation

There's always a reason to smile

TODAY I AM GRATEFUL FOR

1.
2.
3.

TODAY I FELT

HOW I RATE THE DAY

☆ ☆ ☆ ☆

Why I am grateful:
_____
_____
_____
_____
_____
_____

Tomorrow I look forward to:

Priorities:
☐ _____
☐ _____
☐ _____

What I learned today:

Notes to self

Date: _____

Weather:

Today's Date: _____

MY THOUGHTS ABOUT TODAY

Consider: People, places, experiences, activities, accomplishments, surprises, coincidences, ideas, lessons, inspirations, aspirations, appreciation, hopes, fears, feelings, failings, concerns, health, meals, enjoyment, eureka moments...

_____
_____
_____
_____
_____
_____
_____
_____
_____

Today's Affirmation

When I fail I try again

TODAY I AM GRATEFUL FOR

1. _____
2. _____
3. _____

TODAY I FELT

HOW I RATE THE DAY
☆ ☆ ☆ ☆ ☆

Why I am grateful:

_____
_____
_____
_____
_____

Tomorrow I look forward to:

Priorities:

- ☐ _____
- ☐ _____
- ☐ _____

What I learned today:

Notes to self

Date: _____

Weather: ☀ ⛅ ☁ ⛈ 🌧

Other Books from the Author

If you like this journal, chances you'll enjoy my other work - coloring books, journals and activity books, some of which are listed below.

REFLECTIONS
Inspirational Coloring Journal for Women

REFLECTIONS
Inspirational Coloring Journal for Teenage Boys

REFLECTIONS
Inspirational Coloring Journal for Men

REFLECTIONS
Inspirational Coloring Journal for Adults

A range of guided and gratitude journals

A range of Activity Books

A selection of Log Books

Inspirational Coloring Book for Teenage Girls

Inspirational Coloring Book for Teenage Boys

Inspirational Coloring Book for Women

Inspirational Coloring Book for Men

Inspirational Coloring Book for Adults

Inspirational Coloring Book for Boys

Inspirational Coloring Book for Girls

Coloring book for kids aged 4-8

Coloring book for kids aged 2-4

www.ingramcontent.com/pod-product-compliance
Lightning Source LLC
Chambersburg PA
CBHW070044230426
43661CB00005B/759